AN
EASY-READ
FACT
BOOK

Prehistoric Man

Angela Hart

Franklin Watts
London   New York   Toronto   Sydn

© 1983 Franklin Watts Ltd

First published in Great Britain in
    1983 by
Franklin Watts Ltd
12a Golden Square
London W1

First published in the USA by
Franklin Watts Inc.
387 Park Avenue South
New York
N.Y. 10016

UK ISBN: 0 86313 014 3
US ISBN: 0-531-04511-0
Library of Congress Catalog Card
    Number: 82-51002

Printed in Great Britain by
    Cambus Litho, East Kilbride

Photographs supplied by
Imitor

Illustrated by
Eagle Artists
Christopher Forsey
Hayward Art Group
Michael Roffe

Designed and produced by
David Jefferis

Technical consultant
Anne Millard Ph.D

Prehistoric Man

Contents

Man's distant past

Today, Man is the ruling animal on Planet Earth. Yet 14 million years ago, next to no time compared with the 4-billion-year history of the world, there were no people. Our ancestors

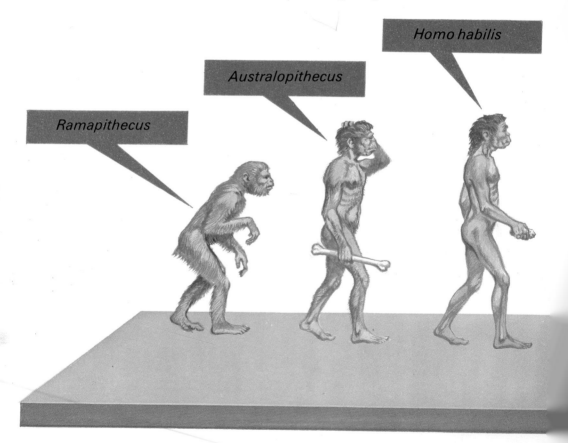

Ramapithecus

Australopithecus

Homo habilis

were ape-like animals living in trees.

Scientists have pieced together our history with great care. Fossils – bones preserved in rocks – give an idea of what our ancestors looked like. Remains of their tools and weapons are clues to the way they lived.

There are still many puzzles. But new discoveries are made each year to add to the story.

▽ Six steps along the path to modern man. These and other ancestors of ours cover a period of more than 14 million years. You will see many of them in this book.

Homo erectus

Neanderthal (Homo sapiens)

Cro-Magnon (Homo sapiens)

Dawn of Mankind

On these pages you can see *Ramapithecus*, the small, ape-like creature that scientists think could have been our ancestor.

Ramapithecus lived in forests between 14 and 6 million years ago. At night it probably slept in the safety of the branches, only climbing down to ground level during the day. Much of the time it scuttled about on all fours. But sometimes it may have stood on its hind legs, perhaps when stretching out to grasp a tasty fruit dangling from a young tree. From this developed one of the main differences between us and other animals – the fact that we walk on two legs rather than four.

Around 14 million years ago there also lived another ape-like creature called *Dryopithecus*. Scientists think that this may have been the ancestor of today's apes.

▷*Ramapithecus*, waking to the rays of the rising sun. The shape of its jaws and teeth are more like those of a human than an ape. This is what makes scientists think that *Ramapithecus* is our ancestor.

On the grassy plains

△ *Australopithecus* enjoying a snack. Like chimpanzees of today, it may have poked twigs into termite nests to get at the tasty grubs inside.

Living in Africa about 3 million years ago were several kinds of man-apes called hominids. The name hominid comes from the word *homo*, which means "man."

One sort of hominid was *Australopithecus* and there were several kinds. The tallest grew no more than 4.9 ft (1.5 m) tall and had a brain about half the size of ours. But they could all walk on their two feet. They ate plants and

fruit and probably stole birds' eggs when they had the chance.

Living at the same time was another hominid called *Homo*. It had a bigger brain than *Australopithecus* and scientists think it was a direct ancestor of man. *Homo* was a meat-eater. Small groups of them probably hunted slow-moving, sick or young animals. They may have used stones or thick branches to kill them.

△ Another hominid is called *Zinjanthropus*. Here you see its skull, found at Olduvai Gorge in East Africa, and an artist's idea of what it may have looked like in the flesh.

9

The first people

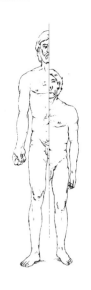

△ *Homo habilis* (right) compared with modern man. As you can see, our ancestor was not very tall.

Very slowly, over millions of years, the hominids developed and changed, until by about 1¾ million years ago the first "men" were walking the world.

Scientists digging up remains in East Africa have found traces of a tool-making ancestor of ours. They named him *Homo habilis* or "handy man." He is thought to be an early member of the bigger group known as *Homo erectus*.

Homo habilis is the first of our ancestors that we know could make and use tools. They were simple stone choppers and sharp stone fragments, but making tools of this type led to the science and technology of today.

Homo habilis also made the first shelters. These were made of twigs and branches, kept in place by rocks and stones. Sleeping at night must have been safer with some protection from the weather and from fierce wild animals such as lions and leopards.

△ No one knew how to make fire, so meat was ripped apart and eaten raw.

▷ A man's hand compared to an ape's. Our thumb helps us to grasp objects firmly and to handle them with skill.

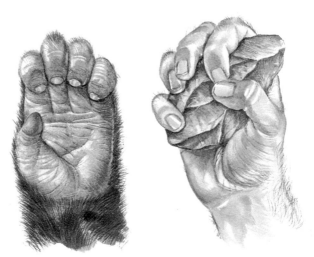

Choppers and axes

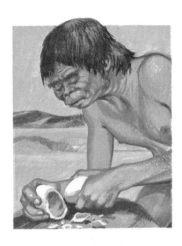

△ *Homo habilis* making a chopper. By carefully splitting it with another rock, the chopper could be shaped quite well.

The sharpened stones which were man's first tools were made some 2 million years ago. Later, hand-axes with sharp pointed ends were made. Later still, about 40,000 years ago, people were making sharp blades from thin slivers of rock.

Making a good hand-axe was a skilled job and no doubt each group had one or two experts who were best at it. First, the right sort of stone had to be found. Then, using another stone as a hammer, the shape of the axe could be roughed out. One wrong blow here could split the stone and the job would have to start again. The sharp edges of the point were made by patient chipping away, probably using an animal bone. The bits of waste stone were useful for slicing meat. Eventually, if all went well, the result would be a pointed hand-axe like the one you can see opposite.

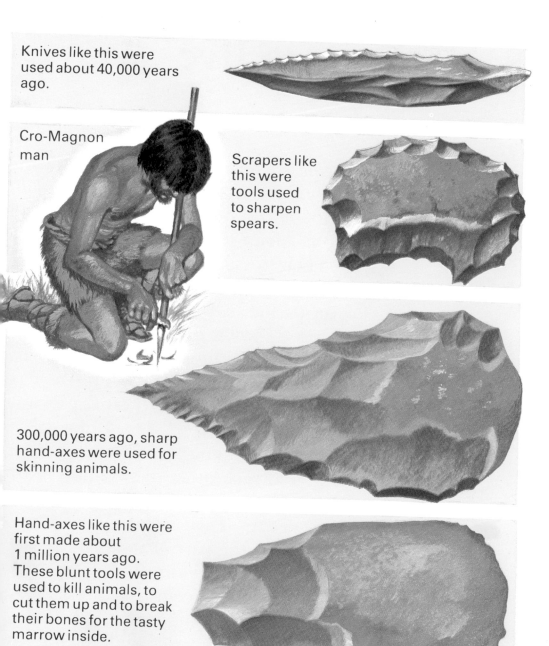

Knives like this were used about 40,000 years ago.

Cro-Magnon man

Scrapers like this were tools used to sharpen spears.

300,000 years ago, sharp hand-axes were used for skinning animals.

Hand-axes like this were first made about 1 million years ago. These blunt tools were used to kill animals, to cut them up and to break their bones for the tasty marrow inside.

* These tools are shown life-size

13

Somewhere to live

△ Simple shelters like this one of branches were made by *Homo habilis* for warmth and to keep out hungry animals.

Homo erectus is the name given to the early form of man to which *homo habilis* belonged. The *erectus* peoples spread from Africa to Europe and Asia.

Their fossil bones, stone tools and other remains show that they lived in groups and had camp-sites. A hut like the one shown opposite was built by *erectus* hunters more than 350,000 years ago, on the beach near present-day Nice in the south of France. It was 29.5 ft (9 m) long.

No one yet knows when people first talked to each other in anything more than shrieks and grunts. From the evidence of *Homo erectus* skulls, we know that the part of the brain which controls speech was well developed by this time. So it seems likely that they had a simple language. This made teamwork easier when building huts or trapping animals such as elephants, antelope or giant baboons.

△ Some people of a *Homo erectus* group, outside their hut in the south of France. There were lots of fish and wild animals to catch here – you can see someone cleaning an animal skin. Perhaps the boy playing with the stick will learn to make it into a spear when he is older.

Conquest of fire

△ A grass fire crackling across the African plains. These two *Homo erectus*, shouting and shrieking, direct terrified animals toward fellow hunters, waiting to spear them for supper.

A roaring grass or forest fire makes all the animals in its way flee with terror. The early hominids must have been frightened too, but at some stage they overcame their fear and took advantage of the flames. They caught fleeing animals and carried them off for food.

The next step was to take a flaming branch and use it to start a fire in the camp. This warmed groups of *Homo erectus* at night and kept away hungry

animals. People could also work by the flickering light, perhaps sharpening stone tools. So the fire became an important meeting-place. Later, fire was used for cooking and for making better tools.

It was a long time before people learned how to make fire themselves. If the camp-fire went out, they had either to wait for another natural fire to start, or perhaps raided a nearby camp.

△ The first cooks were probably *Homo erectus*. Someone must have dropped a piece of meat on the camp-fire and noticed how much tastier it was than raw flesh. From then on it was roast meat on the camp menu!

The long winter

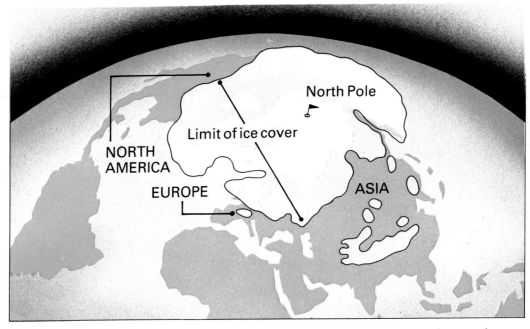

△ The world in the grip of the last Ice Age. Large parts of the Earth were covered in immense ice sheets, hundreds of yards thick.

There are few remains to show how *Homo erectus* gradually developed. But we know that by about 250,000 years ago, a new type of people lived. These were *Homo sapiens*, "wise man," and this is the group to which we also belong.

There were several kinds of *Homo sapiens*. The Neanderthal people were a heavy and stocky type, with strong muscles and sloping foreheads. They lived mainly in Europe at the time of

the last Ice Age, about 50–70,000 years ago. They must have been tough because during this period, much of Europe was covered in ice and snow all the time. Summers were cool and short, winters long and bitterly cold.

The Neanderthals hunted animals such as wolves, bears and woolly mammoths. They used the thick furs as clothes to keep warm, and slept on them as comfy bedding in their cave dwellings.

△ An icy dawn for some Neanderthal hunters. They sought shelter for the night in a small cave, lighting a fire to keep the cold at bay. Perhaps this morning they will be lucky and find the bear they have been tracking for the past two days.

Cave painters

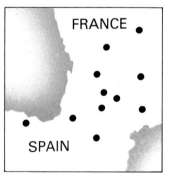

△ This map shows places in France and Spain where Cro-Magnon cave paintings have been found.

The first fully "modern" people of Europe appeared about 40,000 years ago. These early people are called Cro-Magnon, after the place in France where their remains were first found.

We are not sure what happened to the Neanderthals. Cro-Magnons had better tools and weapons and traveled in larger groups. Perhaps they killed off the Neanderthals, or perhaps the Neanderthals could not adapt to the warmer weather as the Ice Age ended.

20

Cro-Magnon people were the world's first artists. They produced magnificent paintings on their cave walls. For paint they used different colored soils mixed with water, and soot for black. Some artists left handprints, others painted pictures of people. But most painted animals and hunting scenes. We do not know whether they are pictures of actual hunts or simply drawn from the artists' imagination.

△ The cave painters drew their pictures in the deepest, darkest parts of their caves. Perhaps there was a magical meaning to them. By painting, say, a bison, an artist might think he would attract a real one to the hunters outside.

A mammoth hunt

The woolly mammoth grew about 9.8 ft (3 m) high and had huge curving tusks. It must have been much prized by the hunters of the Ice Age. For the Cro-Magnons of eastern Europe it provided almost everything. They used its tusks and leg bones to build huts, covered with skins. They dressed in mammoth skins and ate mammoth meat.

The hunting party would leave at dawn. Near their prey, the party split into two. One team attacked the mammoth, driving the injured animal towards the others. These sent a hail of spears, and the animal was doomed, bleeding to death.

Getting the body back home could have been a problem. If camp was fairly near, then other people would come to help hack off the meat. Any left overnight would be eaten by wolves and other wild animals.

△ A cornered mammoth, bleeding from several spear wounds, tries to defend itself from a savage beast – man.

▷ The Cro-Magnons of eastern Europe lived in huts made of mammoth bones and skin.

23

Cro-Magnon life

△ This Cro-Magnon woman is making a jacket. Her needle is made of reindeer antler.

As well as being fine hunters and artists, the Cro-Magnons had many other skills.

They made needles from splinters of reindeer antler to sew together animal skins for clothing. They had no cotton thread, so instead used lengths of leather or gut.

They made many different sorts of tools, including sharp flint knives and flat scrapers for cleaning the grease off animal hides.

The Cro-Magnons loved jewelry. They made beads, bracelets and pendants out of many things, including pebbles, shells and fish bones. We know something of their jewelry as they often had it buried with them when they died.

They also made improvements to weapons. Backward-pointing barbs on spear points made them hold fast into an animal's flesh.

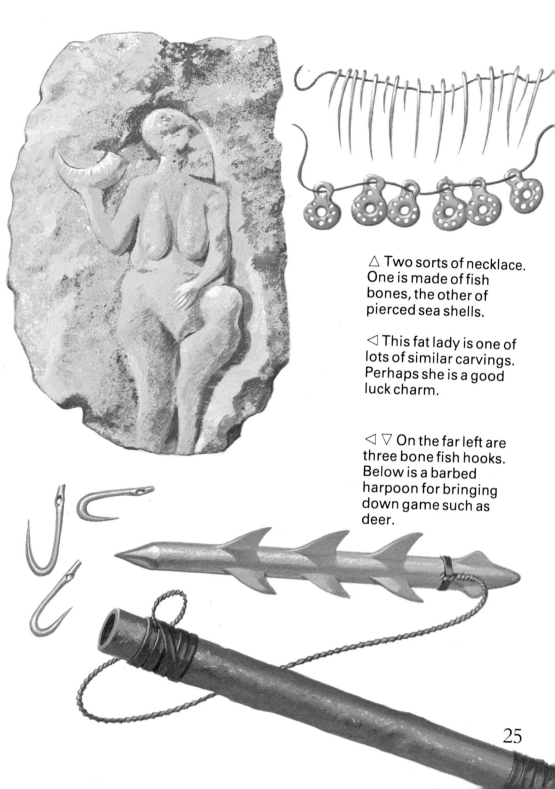

△ Two sorts of necklace. One is made of fish bones, the other of pierced sea shells.

◁ This fat lady is one of lots of similar carvings. Perhaps she is a good luck charm.

◁ ▽ On the far left are three bone fish hooks. Below is a barbed harpoon for bringing down game such as deer.

Farming

About 10,000 years ago the Ice Age was drawing to an end in Europe. About the same time the peoples of the Middle East became the first farmers.

Wheat and barley were the first crops to be cultivated. Wheat grew wild on the hillsides and people collected the seeds and grain. They ground up the grain to make flour for bread. They found that if they sowed the seeds, then young plants would grow. From that discovery it was a short step to growing crops regularly every year.

Goats, sheep, cattle and pigs were tamed and kept for their milk, meat and skins. Hunting wild animals became sport to add variety to the cookpot. It was no longer a daily need.

Now that people stayed in one place to look after their crops and animals, the temporary camp-sites became settled villages. Eventually the villages grew into towns and cities.

▽ This is a farming village of about 10,000 years ago. On the far left you can see wheat being cut by someone using a sickle, a newly invented tool. Goats are the main animals kept in the village. A woman bakes bread, while in front of her someone carries a pitcher of water from a stream. Dogs were now tame – they had been wild just a few thousand years before.

26

◁ This map shows the "fertile crescent," the area in the Middle East where the first farmers lived. The rivers Tigris, Euphrates and Nile were the main sources of fresh water for the area.

MEDITERRANEAN SEA

River Tigris

River Euphrates

River Nile

AFRICA

Finding out about the past

△ This map marks Olduvai Gorge in East Africa. Here, many remains of the very earliest men have been found. Research continues in the area today.

It has taken much careful study to put together our ideas about the development of early man. New discoveries often mean changes in these ideas, so nothing can be taken for granted.

Many remains of the earliest hominids are in East Africa. It is there that scientists think man started to branch away from the rest of the ape family. People later spread all over the world, so scientists work on "digs" in many countries, studying remains of different periods.

Putting a date to these finds can be difficult. The carbon-14 method works well with objects up to 50,000 years old. Radioactive carbon-14 in the air is taken in by plants and the people and animals which eat them. When they die, the carbon-14 slowly decays at a constant rate. By measuring the amount left, scientists can judge how old the remains are.

△ At work uncovering fossil remains. Fossils are the remains of ancient plants, people and animals, preserved in rock.

▷ Remains are often scattered over a wide area. This expert is carefully uncovering a clay gorge, bit by bit, with his pick.

Glossary

Here are explanations of some of the words used in this book and a guide to help you pronounce the names.

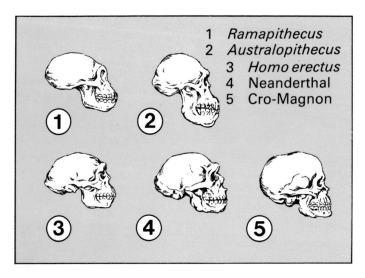

1 *Ramapithecus*
2 *Australopithecus*
3 *Homo erectus*
4 Neanderthal
5 Cro-Magnon

△ These drawings show how man's skull has changed in size and shape. There has been a big increase in brain size and the jaws now thrust forward instead of backward.

Australopithecus
"Southern ape." Early hominid. Its remains have been found in Africa.

Cro-Magnon
People who lived from about 40,000 years ago. They looked similar to modern Europeans.

Dryopithecus
Ancestor of present-day ape family.

Fossil
Remains of prehistoric animals and plants preserved in rock.

Gut
Tough cord made from animal intestines.

Hominid
Name given to the ape-like ancestors of modern man.

Homo erectus
"Upright man." Our ancestors who lived between 1 million and 250,000 years ago.

Homo habilis
"Handy man." Tool-using men who were an early kind of *Homo erectus*.

Homo sapiens
"Wise man." The name for modern man.

Ice Age
Period when the Earth became very cold and ice sheets covered up to one-third of the land.

How to say the names

Cro-Magnon
crow-MAG-non
Dryopithecus
dry-oh-PITHY-kuss
Hominid
HOM-in-id
Homo erectus
Ho-mo ee-REK-tuss
Homo habilis
ho-mo HABY-liss
Homo sapiens
ho-mo SAP-ee-enz
Australopithecus
oss-trall-oh-PITHY-kuss
Ramapithecus
raa-maa-PITHY-kuss
Zinjanthropus
zinj-AN-throw-puss

Our ancestors

Here are some interesting facts about the world of our ancestors.

Neanderthals had a sloping skull and a thick brow ridge which makes them look rather "primitive." Their brain was not primitive, though – it was actually bigger than that of modern man.

Many of the giant animals that survived the Ice Age died out when it ended. Scientists are not sure whether they were hunted to death by early men or whether they could not adapt to a warmer climate. Perhaps both ideas are right.

Until the 19th century, people did not know how old the world was. In 1650, Archbishop Ussher said it was created in 4004 BC. Fossils and other evidence tell scientists that the world is much older – some 3,800 million years in fact.

Recent evidence shows that a 3¾-million-year-old fossil hominid named "Lucy" may be one of the first members of the true human line. This is much earlier than scientists had thought.

The first people crossed to America about 40–25,000 years ago. During this time, so much of the Earth's water was frozen that the sea level around the world fell. Vast stretches of sea bed became dry land. The early men crossed from Asia over the Bering Straits "land bridge." This joined the north-east tip of Asia to what is now the state of Alaska in America.

Index